JOURNEYS

Reader's Notebook

Volume 2

Kindergarten

Houghton Mifflin Harcourt

Contents

Contents

Unit 6

Name _____

is   how

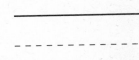

1. The man _____ Sam.

2. _____ can Sam tap?

3. See _____ Sam can tap!

Directions Remind children to write their names. Then have them read each sentence, look at the picture, and write *is* or *how* to complete the sentence. Guide children to capitalize *how* at the beginning of item 2. Then have children read the sentences aloud. Have children point to and name the letters they recognize on the page. Then have them tap their desks once for each word as they read the sentences aloud again. Have children say other sentences with the words *is* or *how*.

Kindergarten, Unit 4

1

Name _____

| of | so | many | where |

1. I see _____  .

2. _____ is Pat?

3. Come with me _____ you can see.

4. Nat is a fan _____ Pat.

Directions Remind children to write their names. Have children read the sentences and look at each picture. Then have them write a word from the box to complete each sentence. Guide children to capitalize *where* in item 2. Then have children read the sentences aloud. Have children point to and name letters they recognize on the page. Then have them tap their desks once for each word as they reread the sentences. Have children say other sentences with *of, so, many,* or *where*.

Words to Know

2

Kindergarten, Unit 4

Name

1.

2.

Directions Remind children to write their names. Then have children name the Alphafriend and its letter. Have them trace and write *I* and *i*. Then help them name the pictures (*igloo, wig, goat,* *ship, car, pin, fish, lips*) and write *Ii* next to the ones whose names contain the short *i* sound.

Remind children to write the upper- and lowercase letters so they can be easily read, using a left-to-right and top-to-bottom progression.

Kindergarten, Unit 4

3

Phonics

Name _____

Words with *i*

1.

pan   pin

2.

Tim   Pam

3.

nap   sit

4.

mat   tip

Directions Remind children to write their names. Then have them look at the first picture, read the words, and circle the word that matches the picture. Repeat with the remaining pictures and words.

Have children say the words that match each picture. Then have them think of words that rhyme with each one.

Phonics

4

Kindergarten, Unit 4

Name _____

Details

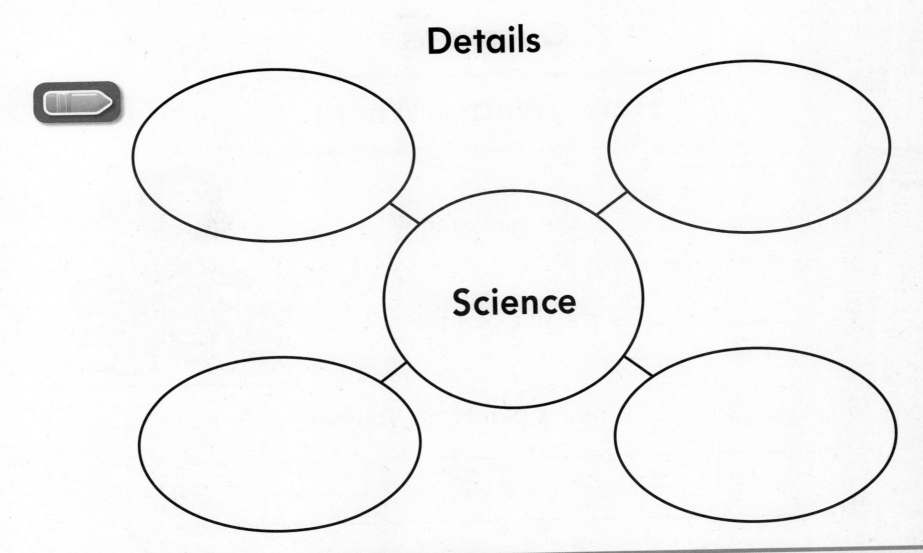

Science

Directions Have children write or draw details they learned from the **Big Book** that tell something about the main idea *Science*.

Have children share their words or pictures with the class. Tell children to speak clearly and to listen carefully as others share.

Kindergarten, Unit 4

Comprehension

Name _____

Questions

How What Where

1. _____ is the girl doing?

2. _____ are the plants?

3. _____ many plants do you see?

4. _____

Name _____

find   this

1. Can you _____ a bat?

2. Is _____ the bat?

3. Can you _____ my hat?

4. _____ is the hat!

Directions Remind children to write their names. Then have them read each sentence, look at the picture, and write *find* or *this* to complete the sentence. Guide children to capitalize *this* at the beginning of item 4. Then have children read the completed sentences aloud. Have children point to and name the letters they recognize on the page. Then have them tap their desks once for each word as they read the sentences aloud again. Have children say other sentences with the words *find* or *this*.

7

Words to Know

Name _____

from came but on

1. A cat _____ to me.

2. Where are you _____ ?

3. I can see _____ this tag.

4. I like you, _____ this is where you live.

Directions Remind children to write their names. Have children read the sentences and look at each picture. Then have them write a word from the box to complete each sentence. Have children read the sentences aloud. Have children point to and name the letters they recognize on the page. Then have them tap their desks once for each word as they reread the sentences. Have children say other sentences with *from, came, but,* and *on.*

Words to Know

8

Kindergarten, Unit 4

Name

1.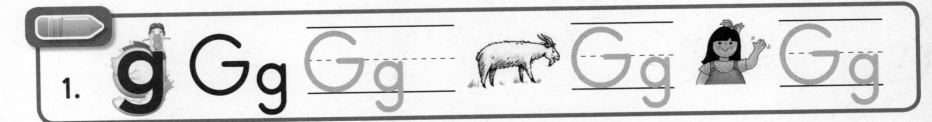
g Gg Gg _____ Gg _____ Gg

2.

Directions Have children name the Alphafriend and its letter. Have them trace and write *Gg*. Then name the pictures together (goat, girl, door, gate, guitar, game, comb, garden). Have children write *Gg* next to the pictures whose names start with the /g/ sound.

Remind children to write the upper- and lowercase letters so they can be easily read.

Phonics

9

Kindergarten, Unit 4

Name _____

Words with *g*

1.

_____ a g

2.

p _____ g

3.

_____ a s

4.

_____ a g

Directions Help children name the pictures (*bag, pig, gas, tag*). Then have them write the missing letter to complete the first picture's name. Repeat with the rest of the pictures and words.

Say pairs of words, some that rhyme with each picture name and others that do not rhyme. Have children raise their hand when they hear a pair of words that rhyme.

Phonics

Kindergarten, Unit 4

Name _____

Sequence of Events

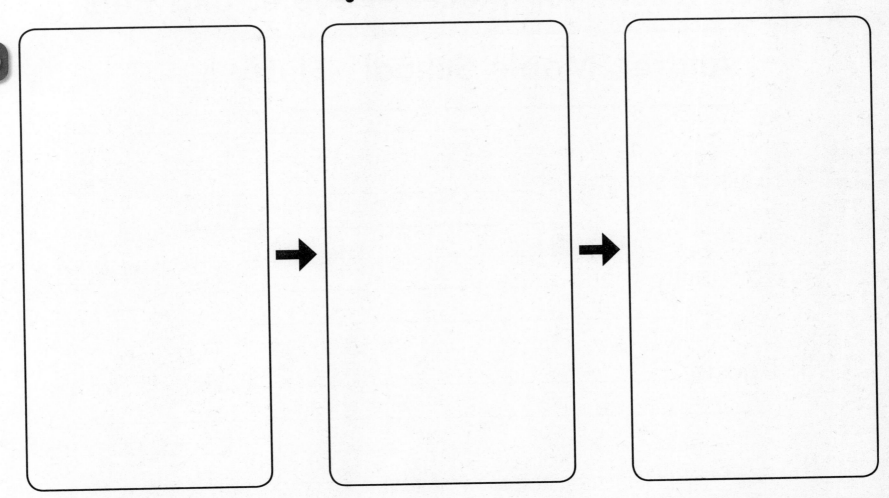

Directions Discuss with children the stages of development from egg to butterfly. Have them draw and label what happens to a caterpillar as it grows into a butterfly.

Have children share their pictures with a group.

11

Comprehension

Name _____

Lesson 17
READER'S NOTEBOOK

From Caterpillar to Butterfly
Grammar: Proper Nouns for Places,
People, and Pets

Proper Nouns for Places, People, and Pets

Andre   Maple School   Fluffy

1. This cat's name is _____.

2. This is my friend _____

3. I go to _____.

4. _____

Name _____

will   be   who

1. _____ will be the cat?

2. Pam will _____ the cat.

3. What will Tim _____?

Directions Remind children to write their names. Have them read each sentence and look at each picture. Then have them write the word *who, will* or *be* to complete each sentence. Guide children to capitalize *who* at the begining of the first sentence. Have children read the completed sentences aloud.

Have children point to and name the letters they recognize on the page. Then have them tap their desks once for each word as they read the sentences aloud again. Have children say other sentences with the words *who, will* or *be*.

Words to Know

13

Name _____

| into | that | your | who |

1. I like _____ cab.

2. Come _____ the cab.

3. Where is _____ hat, Tim?

4. _____ can find it?

Directions Remind children to write their names. Have them read each sentence and look at each picture. Then have them write the word *into, that, your,* or *who* to complete each sentence. Guide children to capitalize *who* at the beginning of the last sentence. Then have children read the sentences aloud. Have children point to and name the letters they recognize on the page. Then have them tap their desks once for each word as they read the sentences aloud again. Have children say other sentences with the words *into, that, your,* and *who.*

Words to Know

14

Kindergarten, Unit 4

Name _____

1.

2.

Directions Have children name the Alphafriend and its letter. Have them trace and write *R* and *r*. Help them name the pictures (*rabbit, ribbon, rat, ship, rug, bird, robot, lip*). Have children write *Rr* next to the pictures whose names start with the /r/ sound.

Help children think of groups of words that begin with the /r/ sound. For example, *Racing rabbits run rapidly.*

15

Phonics

Kindergarten, Unit 4

Words with *r*

1.

cat   rat

2.

rip   sit

3.

ran   rag

4.

mat   ram

Directions Help children name the pictures (rat, rip, ran, ram). Have them circle the word that names the first picture. Repeat with the rest of the pictures and words.

Have children say the words that name each picture. Then have them think of rhyming words for each one.

Name _____

Author's Purpose

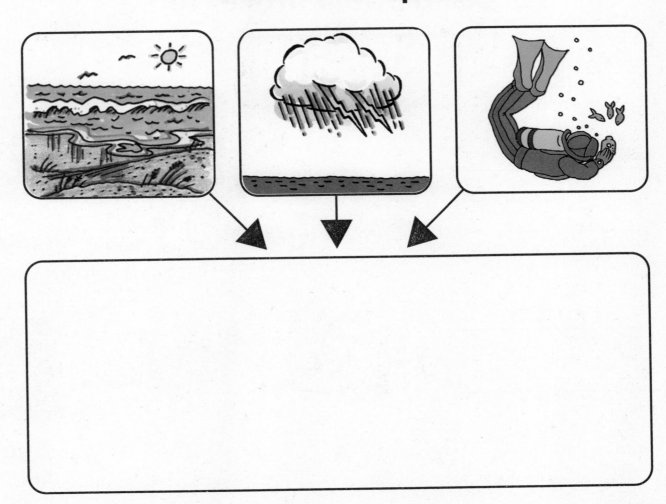

Directions Tell children to look at the pictures in the boxes. Have them draw a picture showing something they think the author wanted them to learn about the Atlantic Ocean.

Discuss with children some of the information in the book. Encourage children to share things they have learned about the ocean.

Comprehension

Kindergarten, Unit 4

Name _____

Verbs in the Future Tense

We   I

1. _____
   _____
   _____

2. _____
   _____
   _____

Directions Have children name each picture. Then have them complete each sentence by writing a word from the box and circling the picture that shows what will happen in the future.

Have children read their sentences aloud using a future-tense verb to describe the picture they circled. Tell them to speak clearly as they share their sentences and to listen carefully to others as they share.

Grammar

18

Kindergarten, Unit 4

Name _____

go   for

1. How can I _____ ?

2. This is sad _____ me.

3. Is this cab _____ me?

4. Now I can _____ !

Directions Remind children to write their names. Next, have children read each sentence and look at the picture. Then have them write the word *go* or *for* to complete each sentence. Have children read the completed sentences aloud.

Remind children to write the letters so they can be easily read, using a left-to-right and top-to-bottom progression.

Words to Know

19

Kindergarten, Unit 4

Name _____

here   they   soon   up

1. I like it _____.

2. Tam and Sam are _____ on the mat.

3. _____ will come here with me.

4. We will go in _____.

Directions Remind children to write their names. Have children read each sentence and look at the picture. Then have them write *here, they, soon,* or *up* to complete each sentence. Guide children to capitalize *they* at the beginning of item 3. Have children read the page aloud. Have children point to and say the names of letters they recognize. Then have them tap their desks once for each word as they read the sentences aloud again. Have children say other sentences with the words *here, they, soon,* and *up*.

Words to Know

Kindergarten, Unit 4

Name _____

1. d Dd Dd

2.

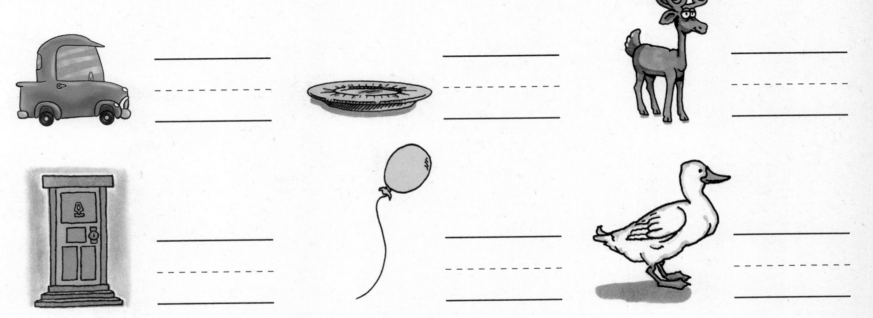

Directions Remind children to write their names. Next, have children name the Alphafriend and its letter. Have them trace and write *D* and *d*. Then help them name the pictures (*dog, doll,* *car, dish, deer, door, ballon, duck*) and write *Dd* next to the ones whose names start with the /d/ sound.

Help children think of groups of words that begin with the /d/ sound. Example: *Dudley Duck digs daisies.*

Phonics

21

Kindergarten, Unit 4

Name _____

Words with *d*

1.

_____ i g

2.

D _____ n

3.

_____ i p

4.

_____ a d

Directions Remind children to write their names. Tell children to look at the first picture and name it. Then have them write the missing letter to complete the picture's name. Repeat with the rest of the pictures and words.

Say pairs of rhyming and non-rhyming words that go with each picture. Have children raise their hands when they hear a pair of words that rhyme.

Phonics

Kindergarten, Unit 4

Name _____

Cause and Effect

Cause	Effect
The sheep get lost.	

Directions Read aloud the cause from the story in the first column, and discuss it with children. Have them draw a picture of an effect, or something that happens because the sheep are lost.

Have children share their pictures with the class and tell about the key event in their pictures.

23

Name _____

Verbs in the Past Tense

You   We

1. _____

2. _____

Directions Have children name each picture. Then have them complete each sentence by writing a word from the box and circling the picture that shows what happened in the past.

Have children read their sentences aloud using a past-tense verb to describe the picture they circled. Tell them to speak clearly as they share their sentences and to listen carefully to others as they share.

Grammar

24

Name _____

| is this will for |

1. This is _____ you.

2. What _____ in the bag?

3. I like _____ cap.

4. It _____ fit me!

Directions Remind children to write their names. Have children read the sentences and look at each picture. Then have them write the correct word from the box to complete each sentence. Have children read the completed sentences aloud.

Have children point to and say the names of letters they recognize on the page. Then have them clap once for each word as they read the sentences aloud again. Have children tell a story using all of the Words to Know.

25

Words to Know

Kindergarten, Unit 4

Name _____

find   your   where   here

_____

1. _____ are you?

2. I will _____ you!

3. I see _____ .

4. _____ you are!

Directions Remind children to write their names. Have children read the sentences and look at each picture. Then have them write a word from the box to complete each sentence. Guide children to capitalize the first letter at the beginning of a sentence. Then have children read the sentences aloud. Have children point to and say the names of letters they recognize on the page. Then have them tap their desks once for each word as they read the sentences aloud again. Have children say other sentences using the Words to Know.

Words to Know

Name

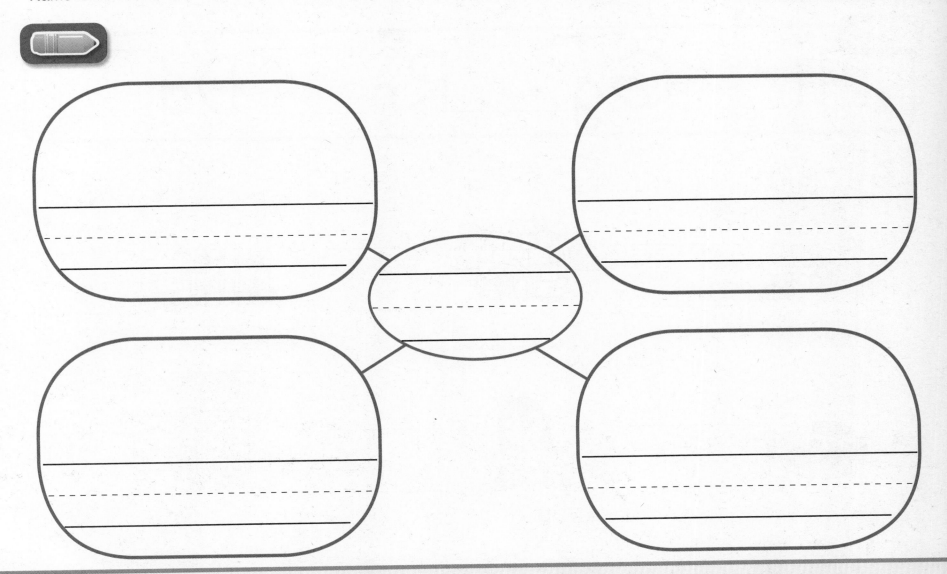

Directions Help children **generate ideas** for their opinion sentences. Have children write ideas and draw pictures for their opinion sentences in the ovals of the graphic organizer. Guide children to write words or draw pictures telling or showing their opinion in the center oval and the reasons for their opinion in the other ovals.

27

Writing

Kindergarten, Unit 4

Name _____

1. Ii _____ Gg _____ Rr _____ Dd _____

2.

 _____

 _____

 _____

 _____

 _____

 _____

Directions Remind children to write their names. Have children name each letter and write *Ii, Gg, Rr,* and *Dd*. Then help children name the pictures (*robot, igloo, gate, insect, girl, door*) and write the capital and lowercase letters for the sound they hear at the beginning of each name.

Remind children to write the letters so they can be easily read, using a left-to-right and top-to-bottom progression.

Phonics

Kindergarten, Unit 4

Name _____

Opinion Sentences

_____

- -

_____

- -

_____

_____

- -

_____

Directions Have children use pages 29–30 to draft, revise, and edit their opinion sentences. Encourage children to use their ideas from **Reader's Notebook** page 27 as a guide in their writing. As children **develop their drafts**, remind them that they will have a chance to add to their sentences on another day. As children **revise their drafts**, discuss words and reasons they could add that would make their opinion sentences even better. As children **edit their drafts**, help them use what they know about letters and sounds to check the spelling of words. Have them check spelling, using other sources as appropriate. Have children also check their sentences for correct capitalization and punctuation.

29

Name _____

Opinion Sentences

_____

- -

_____

_____

- -

_____

_____

- -

_____

Directions Have children use pages 29–30 to draft, revise, and edit their opinion sentences. Encourage children to use their ideas from **Reader's Notebook** page 27 as a guide in their writing. As children **develop their drafts**, remind them that they will have a chance to add to their sentences on another day. As children **revise their drafts**, discuss words and reasons they could add to make their opinion sentences even better. As children **edit their drafts**, help them use what they know about letters and sounds to check the spelling of words. Have them check spelling, using other sources as appropriate. Have children also check their sentences for correct capitalization and punctuation.

Writing

30

Name _____

Review Words with *d*, *g*, *i*, *r*

1.

bag   bin

2.

cat   Dad

3.

pin   pat

4.

man   ram

Directions Remind children to write their names. Then tell children to look at the first picture, read both words, and circle the one that matches the picture. Repeat with the rest of the pictures and words.

Have children say the words that match each picture. Then have them think of words that rhyme with each one.

31

Phonics

Name _____

Sequence of Events

First, George and the man with the yellow hat go to the dinosaur museum.

Next, George goes to the quarry and helps dig for dinosaur bones.

Directions Tell children you will read aloud sentences about the beginning and middle of the story. Have children tell which words in the sentences are about sequences. Have them draw a picture of something that happens at the end of the story.

Have children share their pictures and talk about key events at the end of the story. Then have them retell or act out the ending.

Comprehension

Kindergarten, Unit 4

Name _____

Verbs: Past, Present, Future

| skated   skate   will skate |

_____

1. Yesterday we _____.

_____

2. Today we _____.

_____

3. Tomorrow we _____.

Directions Talk about the picture with children. Then have them complete each sentence by writing a word or words from the box.

Have children read their sentences aloud. Have them tell whether the sentence tells about one or more than one person. Tell them to speak clearly as they share their sentences and to listen carefully to others as they share.

Kindergarten, Unit 4

Name _____

make play

_____

1. We _____ with a bag.

2. I can _____ a pig!

3. I can _____ a cat!

Directions Remind children to write their names. Next, have children read each sentence and look at the picture. Then have them write the word *make* or *play* to complete each sentence. Have children read the completed sentences aloud.

Have children point to and say the names of letters they recognize on the page. Then have children tap their desks once for each word as they read the sentences aloud again. Have children say other sentences with the words *make* or *play*.

Words to Know

34

Name _____

them give say new

 1. These are _____ !

2. You can play with _____ .

3. I will _____ them to you.

4. "We like them," they _____ !

Directions Remind children to write their names. Have children read each sentence and look at the picture. Then have them write *them, give, say,* or *new* to complete each sentence. Have children read the page aloud. Have children point to and say the names of letters they recognize. Then have them tap their desks once for each word as they read the sentences aloud again. Have children say other sentences with the words *them, give, say,* and *new*.

Words to Know

35

Kindergarten, Unit 5

Name _____

1.

2.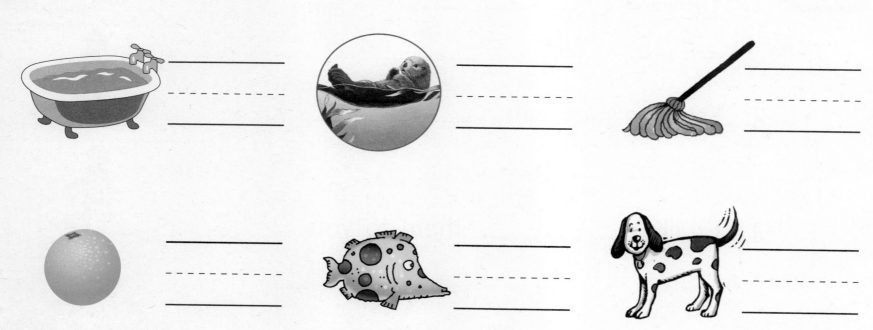

Directions Remind children to write their names. Have children name the Alphafriend and its letter. Next, have them trace and write *O* and *o*. Help children name the pictures (*octopus, ox, pots, tub, otter, mop, orange, fish, dog*). Then have them write *Oo* next to the pictures whose names contain the short *o* sound. Help children think of groups of words that begin with the short *o* sound. For example, *on, opposite, octopus*.

Phonics

36

Kindergarten, Unit 5

Name _____

Words with *o*

1.

dog   dig

2.

mad   mop

3.

pots   bats

4.

dot   cat

Directions Remind children to write their names. Tell children to look at the first picture. Then have them circle the word that names the picture. Repeat with the remaining pictures and words.

Have children read the words they circled. Then have them think of words that rhyme with each one.

Phonics

37

Kindergarten, Unit 5

Name _____

Details

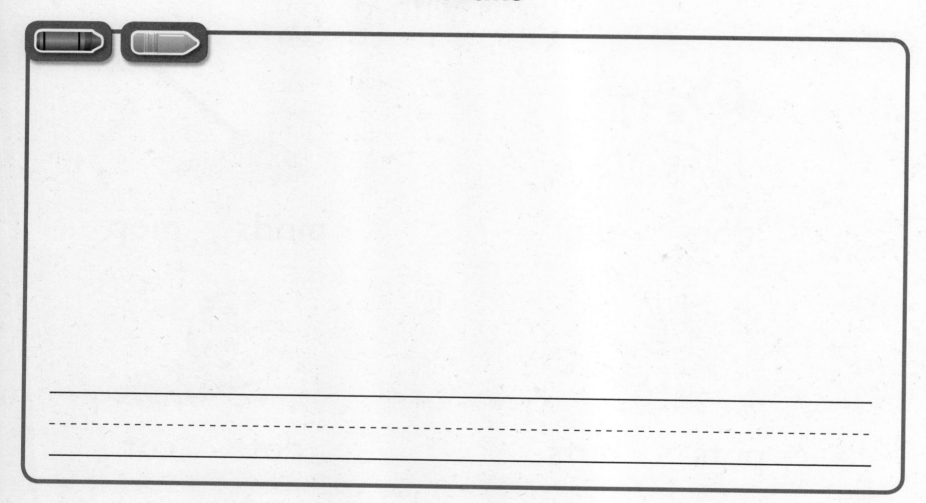

Directions Have children choose an instrument from the
Big Book. Have them draw the instrument in as much detail
as they can.

Then have them write about the instrument or how it is played.

Comprehension

Kindergarten, Unit 5

Name _____

Pronouns *he*, *she*, *we*

We	She	He

1. My sister and I play ball. _____

2. The boy likes to skate. _____

3. The girl is happy. _____

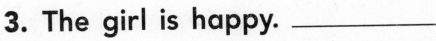

4. _____

Directions Read each sentence with children. Have them write a pronoun from the box to use in place of the nouns. Have children write a list of the pronouns they have learned. Have children write a complete sentence using one of the pronouns.

Have them share their sentences with the class.

39

Grammar

Kindergarten, Unit 5

Name _____

said   good

1. "I can make a _____ dog," I said.

2. "Come and see it."

3. "I like it," Mom _____.

4. "This dog is _____!"

Directions Remind children to write their names. Next have children read the words in the box and talk about each picture. Then have them write the word *said* or *good* to complete each sentence. Have children read the completed sentences aloud.

Have children point to and say the names of letters they recognize on the page. Then have children tap their desks once for each word as they read the sentences aloud again. Have children say other sentences with the words *said* and *good*.

Words to Know

40

Kindergarten, Unit 5

Name _____

| was | then | ate | could |

_____
1. I _____ a fig.

_____
2. The fig _____ so good!

"_____
3. _____ here are many," Mom said.

_____
4. So I ate what I _____!

Directions Remind children to write their names. Have children read each sentence and look at the picture. Then have them write *was, then, ate,* or *could* to complete each sentence. Guide children to capitalize *then* at the beginning of item 3. Have children read the page aloud. Have children point to and say the names of letters they recognize. Then have them tap their desks once for each word as they read the sentences aloud again. Have children say other sentences with the words *was, then, ate,* and *could*.

Words to Know

Kindergarten, Unit 5

Name _____

1.

2.

3.

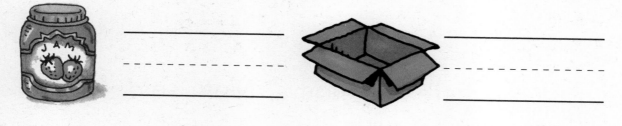

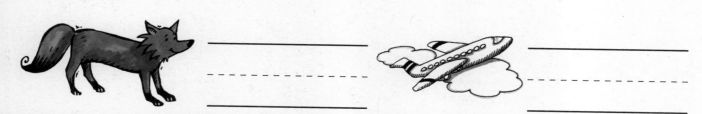

Directions Have children name each Alphafriend and its letter. Have them write *Xx* and *Jj*. Then help children name each picture (ox, ax, jar, jeans, jam, box, fox, jet). Have children write *Jj* when they hear the /j/ sound at the beggining of a picture name and *Xx* when they hear the /ks/ sound at the end of the picture name.

Remind children to write the upper- and lowercase letters so they can be easily read.

Phonics

42

Kindergarten, Unit 5

Name _____

Words with *x, j*

1.

_____

_____ a r

2.

_____

f _____ x

3.

_____

_____ o g

4.

_____

a _____

Directions Tell children to look at the first picture and name it.
(jar) Then have them write the missing letter to complete the
picture's name. Repeat with the rest of the pictures and words,
helping children name the pictures as needed (fox, jog, ax).

Phonics

Kindergarten, Unit 5

Name _____

Story Structure

Characters: Leo, his family and friends	**Setting:** Inside and Outside Leo's house
Problem: Leo hasn't bloomed. **Solution:**	

Name _____

Pronouns *they*, *it*, *I*

| They   It   I |

1. The flower is red. _____

_____

2. The children play soccer. _____

3. Mary can read. _____

_____

4. _____

Directions Read each sentence with children. Have them write a pronoun from the box to use in place of the nouns. Then have children dictate or write a list of the pronouns they have learned.

Have children write a complete sentence using one of the pronouns from the list. Have them share their sentences with the class.

45

Grammar

Kindergarten, Unit 5

Name _____

she   all

_____

1. Can we _____ fit?

2. _____ will sit.

_____

3. Now we can _____ fit!

Directions Remind children to write their names. Have children read the words in the box and look at each picture. Then have them write *she* or *all* to complete each sentence. Guide children to capitalize *she* at the beginning of item 2. Have children read the page aloud.

Have children point to and say the names of letters they recognize. Then have children tap their desks once for each word as they read the sentences aloud again. Have children say other sentences with the words *she* and *all*.

Words to Know

46

Kindergarten, Unit 5

_____

Name _____

over   her   when   some

 **1.** Can Tab go _____ it?

2. _____ will she go?

3. Tab got _____ tag in!

4. Tab will find _____  !

Directions Remind children to write their names. Then have children read each sentence and look at the picture. Then have them write the word *over, her, when,* or *some* to complete each sentence. Guide children to capitalize *when* at the beginning of item 2. Have children read the page aloud. Have children point to and say the names of letters they recognize. Then have them tap their desks once for each word as they read the sentences aloud again. Have children say other sentences with the words *over, her, when,* and *some.*

47

Words to Know

Kindergarten, Unit 5

Name _____

1. E e   E e _____ _____

2.

 _____

 _____

 _____

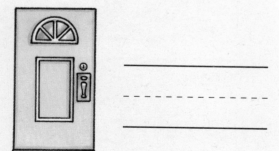 _____

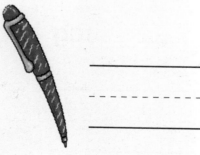 _____

 _____

Directions Have children write their name at the top of the page. Have them name the Alphafriend and its letter. Have children trace and write *E* and *e*. Then help children name the pictures (egg, bed, elbow, vine, net, door, pen, hen). Have children write *Ee* next to the pictures whose names contain the /ĕ/ sound. Then have children say whether they hear /ĕ/ at the beginning or in the middle of a picture name.

Phonics

48

Kindergarten, Unit 5

Name _____

Words with *e*

1.

bed **bad**

2.

pin **pen**

3.

ten **net**

4.

net **bat**

Directions Tell children to look at the first picture. Then have them circle the word that names the picture. Repeat with the remaining pictures and words.

Have children read the words that name each picture. Then have them think of words that rhyme with each of the words.

49

Phonics

Kindergarten, Unit 5

Sequence of Events

First, Zinnia digs in the soil and plants seeds.

↓

Next, Zinnia waters the seedlings and pulls weeds.

↓

Directions Reread aloud pages 4, 6, and 12 of the **Big Book**. Have children pantomine the series of actions. Then tell children you will read sentences about the beginning and middle of the story. Have them identify the sequence words. Ask them to draw a picture of what happens last. Then have them share pictures, pointing out key event(s) from the story's end. Have them retell or act out the story, using the words *first, next,* and *last*. Display page 26. Have children tell why Zinnia has signs there.

Name _____

Proper Nouns for Days and Months

1. We play ball on saturday.

2. We swim in august.

3.

4.

Directions Read the sentences aloud with children. Have children circle the beginning letter of the word that names a day or a month. Then have them tell whether the letter is written correctly. Have children write each sentence correctly.

Read the sentences aloud with children. Then ask children to use separate paper to write and illustrate an invitation to a friend, using one of the sentences above.

Grammar

Kindergarten, Unit 5

Name _____

he   no

1. _____ can get a pet.

2. Dad said _____ to the dog.

3. Dad said _____ to the pig.

4. This is what _____ can get.

Directions Remind children to write their names. Have children read the words in the box and look at each picture. Then have them write *he* or *no* to complete each sentence. Guide children to capitalize *he* at the beginning of item 1. Then have children read the page aloud. Have children point to and say the names of letters they recognize. Then have children tap their desks once for each word as they read the sentences aloud again. Have children say other sentences with the words *he* and *no*.

Words to Know

Kindergarten, Unit 5

Name _____

| away | must | by | there |

1. The man will go _____ soon.

2. This man _____ get in.

3. He will not get _____.

4. He can go _____ cab!

Directions Remind children to write their names. Then have children read each sentence and look at the picture. Then have them write the word *away, must, by,* or *there* to complete each sentence. Have children read the page aloud. Have children point to and say the names of letters they recognize. Then have them tap their desks once for each word as they read the sentences aloud again. Have children say other sentences with the words *away, must, by,* and *there.*

53

Words to Know

Kindergarten, Unit 5

Name _____

1.

2.

3.

Directions Have children name each Alphafriend and its letter.
Have them write *Hh* and *Kk*. Then help children name each
picture (hat, house, king, kite, helicopter, keys, kitten, hand).
Have children write *Hh* when they hear the /h/ sound and *Kk*
when they hear the /k/ sound in a picture name. Remind
children to write the upper- and lowercase letters so they can be
easily read.

Name _____

Words with *h, k*

1.

h ___ n

2.

___ i t

3.

h o ___

4.

___ a t

Directions Tell children to look at the first picture and name it. (hen) Then have them write the missing letter to complete the picture's name. Help children name the remaining pictures (kit, hot, hat). Guide them as needed to write the letter needed to complete each picture name. Say pairs of rhyming and non-rhyming words for each picture. Then have children raise their hand when they hear a pair of words that rhyme.

Phonics

55

Kindergarten, Unit 5

Conclusions

| The first chameleon has friendly colors. | The other chameleon sees the first chameleon. | The other chameleon sees that the first chameleon is friendly. |

Directions Tell children you are going to read aloud sentences with details from the **Big Book**. Have them draw a picture of what they think will likely happen.

Have children share and tell classmates about their pictures. Discuss with children how they used what they knew from the **Big Book** when they drew something that could happen next.

Name _____

Questions

1. is the balloon

2. can you jump

3.  _____

4.  _____

Directions Read the first two items aloud with children. Have children circle the happy face if the question is a complete sentence and the sad face if it is not.

Then help children rewrite each question correctly. Help them make the first item a complete question. Then guide them to change the beginning letter of the first word to a capital letter and add a question mark to the end of each question. Read the questions aloud with children.

Grammar

Kindergarten, Unit 5

Name _____

all   he   no   she

1. Is it _____ for me?

2. _____, it is not.

3. _____ will get a bit.

4. _____ will get a bit.

Directions Remind children to write their names. Have children read the words in the box and look at each picture. Then have them write the word *all*, *he*, *no*, or *she* to complete each sentence. Guide children to capitalize the first letter at the beginning of items 1, 2, and 3.
Have children read the completed sentences aloud.
Then have them tell a story using *all*, *no*, *he* and *she*.

Words to Know

58

Kindergarten, Unit 5

Name _____

| play   make   must   by |

1. There will be a _____ .

2. We can _____ a set.

3. It _____ be a hit!

4. Come _____ and see it!

New Play Soon

Directions Remind children to write their names. Then have children read each sentence and look at the picture. Have them write *play, make, must,* or *by* to complete each sentence. Next, have children read the page aloud. Have children point to and say the names of letters they recognize. Then have them tap their desks once for each word as they read the sentences aloud again. Have children say other sentences with the words *play, make, must,* and *by.*

Words to Know

Kindergarten, Unit 5

Name _____

K	W	L

My Sources

Directions Help children **generate ideas** for their report. Have them write and draw pictures showing what they already know about their topics in the box labeled *K*. Then help them generate and write questions about this topic in the box labeled *W*. Have children circle the sources they will use to answer their questions. After children have gathered evidence about their topic, have them write or draw these facts in the box labeled *L*. Tell children that this week they will use these facts to write a report.

Writing

60

Name _____

O o _____   X x _____   J j _____

E e _____   H h _____   K k _____

 _____

 _____

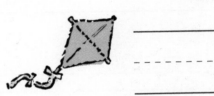 _____

 _____

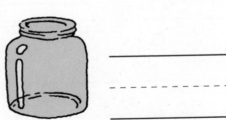 _____

 _____

Directions Have children name each letter. Have them write *Oo, Xx, Jj, Ee, Hh,* and *Kk*. Then help children name the pictures (*helicopter, elbow, kite, keys, jar, otter*). Have children write the letter that stands for the sound at the beginning of each picture name.

Remind children to write the upper- and lowercase letters so they can be easily read.

61

Phonics

Kindergarten, Unit 5

Name _____

My Report

Directions Have children use pages 62–63 to draft, revise and edit a report. Encourage children to use their ideas from **Reader's Notebook** page 60 as a guide in their writing. As children **develop their drafts,** remind them that they will have a chance to add to their report on another day. As children **revise their drafts,** discuss sentences and details they could add to make their reports even better. Have them make sure that they included all of their ideas about the topic. As children **edit their drafts,** help them use what they know about letters and sounds to check the spelling of words. Have them check spelling using other sources as appropriate. Have children also check their sentences for correct capitalization and punctuation.

Kindergarten, Unit 5

Name

My Report

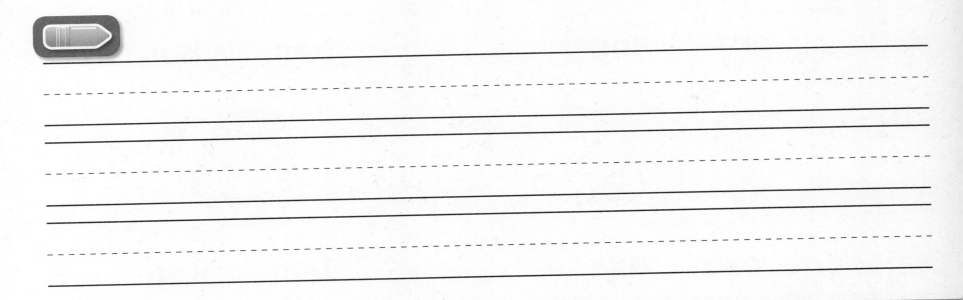

Directions Have children use pages 62–63 to draft, revise and edit a report. Encourage children to use their ideas from **Reader's Notebook** page 60 as a guide in their writing. As children **develop their drafts,** remind them that they will have a chance to add to their report on another day. As children **revise their drafts,** discuss sentences and details they could add to make their reports even better. Have them make sure that they included all of their ideas about the topic. As children **edit their drafts,** help them use what they know about letters and sounds to check the spelling of words. Have them check spelling using other sources as appropriate. Have children also check their sentences for correct capitalization and punctuation.

Kindergarten, Unit 5

Writing

Name _____

Review Words with *o, x, j, e, h, k*

1.

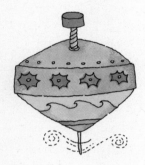

pot   top

2.

pen   hen

3.

ox   ax

4.

Jen   Ken

Directions Help children name the pictures on the page (top, pen, ox, Jen). Tell children to look at the first picture. Have them circle the word that names the picture. Repeat with the remaining pictures and words.

Have children read the words they circled. Then have them think of words that rhyme with each one.

Phonics

Kindergarten, Unit 5

Name _____

Text and Graphic Features

Text/Graphic Feature	Purpose
the part of the recipe on the potholder	

Directions Discuss with children that part of the pie recipe is shown as a text and graphic feature in the book. Have children draw pictures in the second column that show steps in the recipe. Then have children explain how to make a pie using their pictures.

Prompt them to use sequence words they know (*first, next, then,* and *last*) in their descriptions. Discuss with children how paying attention to text and graphic features can help them better understand what they read.

Comprehension

Kindergarten, Unit 5

Exclamations

1. the nest

2. we love birthday cake

3. _____

4. _____

Directions Read the first two items aloud with children. Have children circle the happy face if the exclamation is complete and the sad face if it is not.

Then help children rewrite each exclamation correctly. Help them make the first item a complete exclamation. Then guide them to change the beginning letter of the first word to a capital letter and add an exclamation point to the end. Read the exclamations aloud with children.

Name _____

do   down

 **1.** Jan is at the top.

2. What will Jan _____ now?

3. Jan will go _____!

Directions Remind children to write their names. Have children read the words in the box and look at each picture. Then have them write the word *do* or *down* to complete each sentence. Have children read the completed sentences aloud.

Have children point to and say the names of letters they recognize on the page. Then have them tap their desks once for each word as they read the sentences aloud again. Have children say other sentences with the words *do* or *down*.

Kindergarten, Unit 6

Words to Know

Name _____

went	only	little	just

1. I _____ to see Meg.

2. Meg is my _____ pet.

3. I give Meg a _____ bit.

4. She _____ ate it all!

Directions Remind children to write their names. Have children read the sentences and look at each picture. Then have them write the word *went, only, little,* or *just* to complete each sentence. Have children read the sentences aloud.

Have children point to and say the names of letters they recognize on the page. Then have them tap their desks once for each word as they read the sentences aloud again. Have children say other sentences with the target words.

Words to Know

68

Kindergarten, Unit 6

Name _____

1.

2.

Directions Have children write their names. Have them name the Alphafriend and its letter and trace *U, u*. Identify the pictures (*tub, sun, rug, nut, potato, cub, mug, fan*) and have children write *Uu* next to the pictures whose names contain the short *u* sound.

Remind children to write the upper- and lowercase letters so they can be easily read, using a left-to-right and top-to-bottom progression.

Kindergarten, Unit 6

Phonics

Name _____

Words with *u*

1.

cub   cab

2.

not   nut

3.

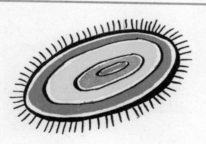

rug   rag

4.

cup   cap

Directions Remind children to write their names. Tell children to look at the first picture. Then have them circle the word that names the picture. Repeat with the rest of the pictures and words.

Have children say the word that names each picture and think of words that rhyme with it.

Phonics

Kindergarten, Unit 6

Name _____

Conclusions

Kitten tries to lick the moon. Kitten tries to chase the moon.	Kitten still can't reach the moon after climbing to the top of a tree.	Kitten sees something big, white, and round, in the pond.

Directions Tell children you are going to read aloud the sentences about the **Big Book**. Have them draw a picture to show why things happen as they do in the story.

Have children use their pictures to discuss their ideas about the story. Encourage them to share how they used what they know and story clues to make their drawings.

Comprehension

Kindergarten, Unit 6

Nouns: Singular and Plural

1.  bear   bears

2.  mitt   mitts

3. fox   foxes

4. _____

Name _____

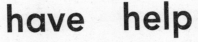
have   help

1. Will you _____ me?

2. I _____ a rag.

3. I _____ a mop.

4. We can all _____!

Directions Remind children to write their names. Have children read the words in the box, look at each picture, and write *have* or *help* to complete each sentence. Then have children read the page aloud.

Have children point to and say the names of letters they recognize on the page. Then have them tap their desks once for each word as they read the sentences aloud again. Have children make up other sentences with *have* or *help*.

Words to Know

Kindergarten, Unit 6

Name _____

one   every   ask   walk

1. Who will go on a _____ with me?

2. I _____ Mom and Dad.

3. "We can go on _____," they say.

4. I like _____ bit of it!

Directions Remind children to write their names. Have children read each sentence, look at the picture, and write a word from the top box to complete the sentence. Have children read the page aloud.

Have children name letters they recognize on the page. Then have them tap their desks once for each word as they read the sentences aloud again. Have children make up other sentences with *one, every, ask,* and *walk*.

Words to Know

Kindergarten, Unit 6

Name _____

1.

2.

3.

Kindergarten, Unit 6

75

Name _____

Words with *l*, *w*

1.

_____ o g

2.

_____ e g

3.

_____ i g

4.

_____ e b

Directions Remind children to write their names. Help children name the pictures. Then have them write the missing letter to complete each picture's name and read the word aloud.

For each picture, say pairs of rhyming and non-rhyming words. Have children raise their hands when they hear a pair of words that rhyme.

Name _____

Compare and Contrast

The big sisters are older.

The big sisters can do things by themselves.

The little sister is younger.

The little sister has to stay home with her parents sometimes.

Directions Tell children you are going to read aloud some sentences that tell how the sisters in the story are different. Then have children draw a picture of how the sisters are alike.

Have children share their pictures with a partner. Have partners discuss their pictures as well as other ways that the sisters in the story are alike.

Comprehension

Kindergarten, Unit 6

Name _____

Subject-Verb Agreement (Past, Present, Future)

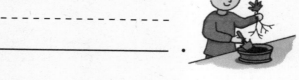

sing   walked   will grow

1. The plant _____ .

2. The children _____ .

3. They _____ .

Directions Have children tell what is happening in each picture. Read the sentence frames and the words in the box aloud with children. Help children identify if the subject of the sentence is talking about one or more than one. Then help them complete the sentences with the appropriate forms of the verbs from the box. Read the completed sentences aloud with children.

Name _____

look out

1. Come _____ at my pet.

2. Can it get _____?

3. It will not get _____ now.

Directions Remind children to write their names. Have children read the words in the box and look at each picture. Then have them write the word *look* or *out* to complete each sentence. Have children read the completed sentences aloud.

Have children point to and say the names of letters they recognize on the page. Then have them clap once for each word as they read the sentences aloud again. Have children say other sentences with the words *look* or *out*.

79

Words to Know

Kindergarten, Unit 6

Name _____

---

very their saw put

1. Where are _____ ?

2. I _____ them there.

3. They are _____ little.

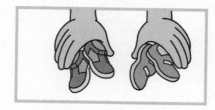

4. I will _____ them on.

Directions Remind children to write their names. Have children read the sentences and look at each picture. Then have them write the word *very, their, saw,* or *put* to complete each sentence. Have children read the sentences aloud. Next, have children point to and say the names of letters they recognize on the page. Then have them tap their desks once for each word as they read the sentences aloud again. Have children say other sentences with the words *very, their, saw,* and *put*.

80

Kindergarten, Unit 6

Name _____

1.

2.

3.

Directions Have children write their names at the top of the page. Have them name each Alphafriend and its letter and trace the letters in rows 1 and 2. Then name the pictures (*vase, vest, zipper, zigzag, zebra, vine, van, zoo*) and have children write

Vv or *Zz* next to the pictures whose names start with the /v/ or /z/ sound. Remind children to write the letters so they can be easily read, using a left-to-right and top-to-bottom progression.

81

Kindergarten, Unit 6

Phonics

Words with *v, z*

1.

van   bat

2.

zip   pin

3.

zig   pig

4.

vet   met

Directions Remind children to write their names. Tell children to look at each picture and read the two words below it. Then have them circle the word that matches the picture. Have children take turns rereading the circled words.

Next, have children choose words from the page and think of words that rhyme with each one.

Phonics
© Houghton Mifflin Harcourt Publishing Company. All rights reserved.

Kindergarten, Unit 6

Name _____

Story Structure

Characters:	**Settings:**
George	museum, restaurant, forest

Beginning: First, George decides to find out what he does best.

Middle: Next, George tries cooking, sledding, and flying a kite.

End:

Have children draw a picture of what happens at the end of the story. Have children share their pictures. Have them retell or act out the event they drew.

Comprehension
© Houghton Mifflin Harcourt Publishing Company. All rights reserved.

Kindergarten, Unit 6

Name _____

Lesson 28
READER'S NOTEBOOK

You Can Do It, Curious George!
Grammar: Subject-Verb Agreement
(Past, Present, Future)

Subject-Verb Agreement (Past, Present, Future)

| will   fetch   naps   roared |

1. The cat _____ .

2. The dog _____ .

3. The lion _____ .

Directions Have children tell what is happening in each picture. Together with children, read aloud the sentence frames and words in the box. Have children complete each sentence by writing the correct word or words from the box. Then read aloud the completed sentences with children.

Have them name the word that tells what the sentence is about. Have them tell whether the sentence tells about one or more than one.

Grammar

Kindergarten, Unit 6

Name _____

off   take

1. We _____ Bud to the tub.

2. Can we get the mud _____?

3. We can not get the mud _____.

4. This will _____ the mud off!

Have children say other sentences using both of the Words to Know. Then have children point to and say the names of letters they recognize.

Words to Know

Kindergarten, Unit 6

Name _____

our day too show

1. This is _____ pet.

2. One _____ he will come with me.

3. I will _____ him to Pat.

4. Ted will pet him, _____.

Directions Remind children to write their names. Have children read each sentence, look at the picture, and write the word *our*, *day*, *too*, or *show* to complete the sentence. Have children read the page aloud. Next, have children point to and say the names of letters they recognize on the page. Then have them tap their desks once for each word as they reread the sentences aloud. Have children say other sentences with the words *our*, *day*, *too*, or *show*.

Words to Know

Kindergarten, Unit 6

Name _____

1. Y y Y y 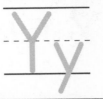 _____ _____

2. Q q Q q  _____ _____

3.

 _____

 _____

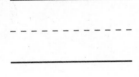 _____

 _____

Directions Have children write their names at the top of the page. Have them name each Alphafriend and its letter and trace the letters in rows 1 and 2. Then name the pictures (*yak, yarn, quilt, quarter, question mark, yard, yolk, queen*) and have children write *Yy* or *Qq* next to the pictures whose names start with /y/ or /kw/. Remind children to write the letters so they can be easily read, using a left-to-right and top-to-bottom progression.

Phonics

87

Kindergarten, Unit 6

Name _____

Words with *y, qu*

1.

_____

_ _ _ _ _ _
____ a k

2.

_____

_ _ _ _ _
____ ip

3.

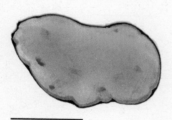

_____

_ _ _ _ _ _
____ a m

4.

_____

_ _ _ _ _ _
____ i z

Directions Remind children to write their names. Tell children to look at the first picture and name it. Then have them write the missing letters to complete the picture's name. Repeat with the rest of the pictures and words, and then have children take turns reading the page.

For each picture, say a mix of rhyming and non-rhyming words. Have children raise their hands when they hear words that rhyme with the picture name.

Phonics

Kindergarten, Unit 6

Name _____

Main Idea and Details

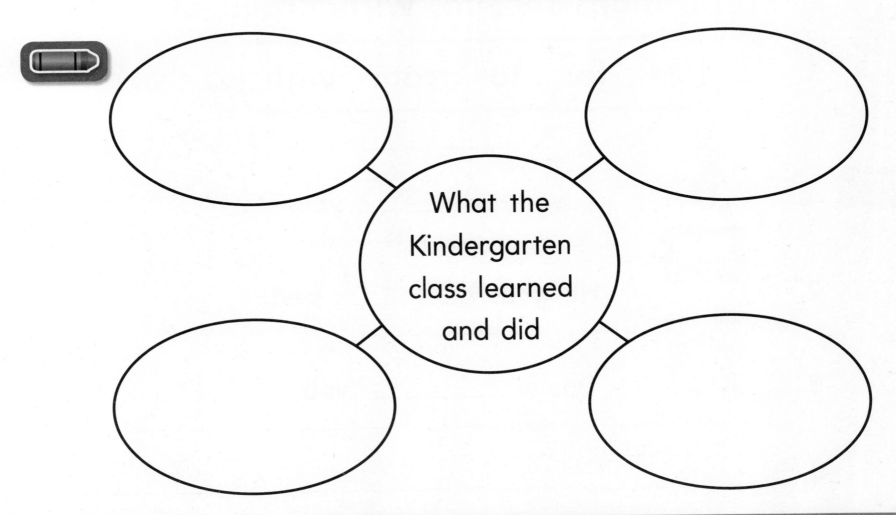

Directions Read aloud the main idea in the center of the web. Have children write or draw details in the **Big Book** that go with the main idea.

Have children share their work with the class. Remind children to speak clearly and to listen carefully as others share.

Comprehension

Kindergarten, Unit 6

Name _____

Prepositions **for**, **to**, **with**, **from**, **of**

of   for   to   from   with

1.   I walk _____ you.

2.   He goes _____ bed.

3.   This is _____ you.

4. _____

Directions Discuss the pictures with children and read each sentence frame aloud. Have children complete each sentence frame by writing a preposition from the box.

Have children write a complete sentence using one of the prepositions they did not use in the sentences. Have them begin the sentence with a capital letter and end it with a period. Have them share their sentences with the class.

Name _____

| do   down   help   look |

 **1.** See what I can _____ .

2. I tap the peg _____ .

3. Now Dad will _____ .

4. Take a _____ at what we did!

Have children reread the words in the box and identify the position word (*down*). Then have them point to and say the names of letters they recognize on the page. Have them say other sentences using the Words to Know.

Kindergarten, Unit 6

Name _____

| walk   little   only   out |

1. My _____ sis is one.

2. She can _____ say "Mom!"

3. Mom will get my sis _____.

4. One day she will _____.

Directions Remind children to write their names. Have children read the sentences and look at each picture. Then have them write a word from the box to complete each sentence. Have children read the sentences aloud. Next, have children point to and say the names of letters they recognize on the page. Then have them tap their desks once for each word as they read the sentences aloud again. Have children say other sentences using the Words to Know.

Words to Know

92

Kindergarten, Unit 6

Name

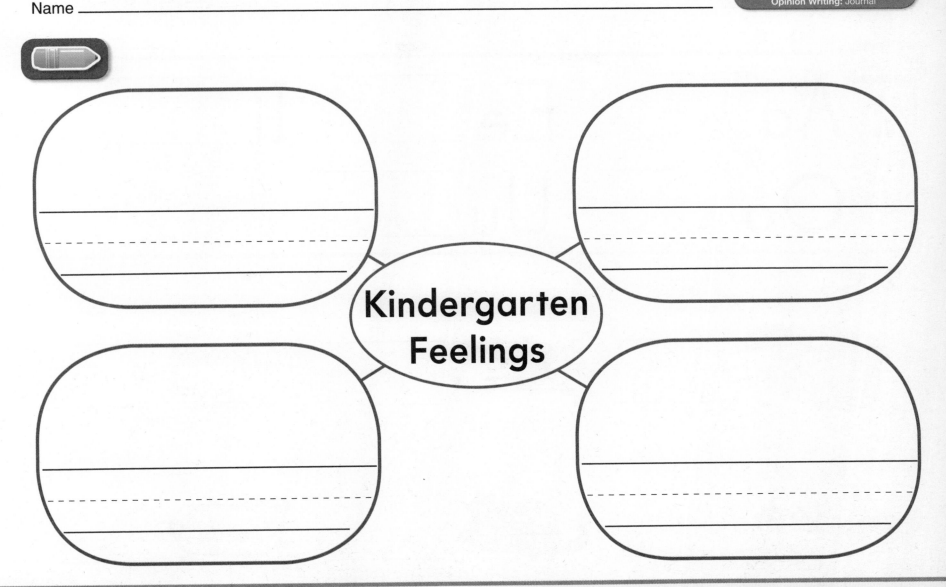

Kindergarten Feelings

Name _____

1.

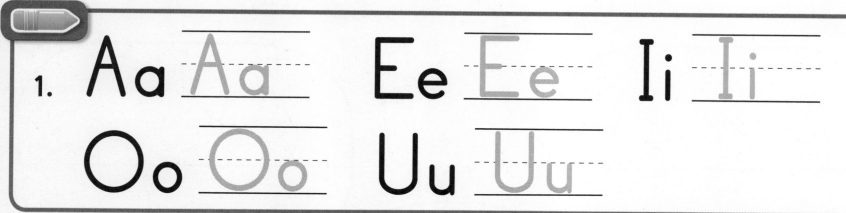

Aa Aa   Ee Ee   Ii Ii

Oo Oo   Uu Uu

2.

Directions Have children write their names at the top of the page. Have them name and trace the letters. Then tell children to name the pictures (*bed, pot, pig, map, dog, tub*) and write the letter for the sound they hear in the middle of each picture name.

Remind children to write the upper- and lowercase letters so they can be easily read, using a left-to-right and top-to-bottom progression.

Phonics

Kindergarten, Unit 6

Name _____

My Journal

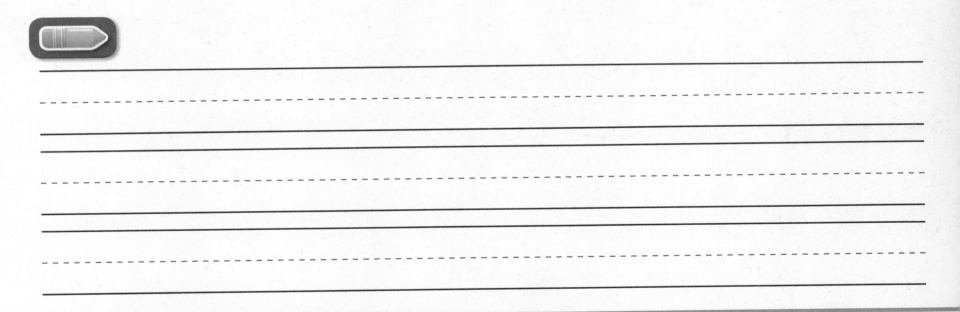

Directions Have children use pages 95–96 to draft, revise, and edit a journal entry. Encourage children to use their ideas from **Reader's Notebook** page 93 as a guide in their writing. As children **develop their drafts**, remind them that they will have a chance to add to their journal entry on another day. As children **revise their drafts**, discuss sentences and details they could add to make their journal entries even better. Have them make sure that they supported their opinions with reasons. As children **edit their drafts**, help them use what they know about letters and sounds to check the spelling of words. Have them check spelling using other sources as appropriate. Have children also check their sentences for correct capitalization and punctuation.

Writing

Kindergarten, Unit 6

Name _____

My Journal

Directions Have children use pages 95–96 to draft, revise, and edit a journal entry. Encourage children to use their ideas from **Reader's Notebook** page 93 as a guide in their writing. As children **develop their drafts**, remind them that they will have a chance to add to their journal entry on another day. As children **revise their drafts**, discuss sentences and details they could add to make their journal entries even better. Have them make sure that they supported their opinions with reasons. As children **edit their drafts**, help them use what they know about letters and sounds to check the spelling of words. Have them check spelling using other sources as appropriate. Have children also check their sentences for correct capitalization and punctuation.

Writing

Kindergarten, Unit 6

Name _____

Words with Short Vowels

1.

yak   lip

2.

vet   web

3.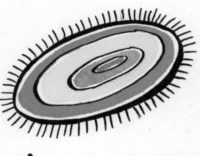

rig   rug

4.

zap   zip

Directions Remind children to write their names. Tell children to look at the first picture. Then have them read the words and circle the one that matches the picture. Repeat with the rest of the pictures and words.

Have children say the words that match each picture and name the vowel sound. Then have them think of words that rhyme with each circled word.

Lesson 30
READER'S NOTEBOOK

Miss Bindergarten Celebrates the
Last Day of Kindergarten
Comprehension: Understanding
Characters

Name _____

Understanding Characters

Character's Behavior	Character's Feelings
Mrs. Bindergarten looks back into the empty classroom as she is leaving on the last day of school.	

Directions Tell children you are going to read aloud a sentence about a character in the story. Have them draw a picture of how they think Miss Bindergarten feels about the last day of school.

Have children share their pictures and talk about how Miss Bindergarten feels. Have them name and tell something about another character from the story. Remind them to speak clearly and loudly enough to be heard.

Comprehension

98

Kindergarten, Unit 6

Name _____

Prepositions **in, on, out, off, by**

in   on   out   off   by

1. The books are _____ the shelf.

2. The bird was in. Now it is _____ .

3. Soup is _____ the bowl.

4. _____

Directions Discuss the pictures with children and read each sentence frame aloud with children. Have children complete each sentence frame by writing a word from the box on the line.

Then have children write a complete sentence using one of the remaining words. Have them begin the sentence with a capital letter and end it with a period. Have children share their sentences with the class. Have them identify the prepositions in their sentences.

Grammar

Kindergarten, Unit 6

many	is
where	how
find	of
this	so

will	from
be	came
into	but
that	on

here	your
they	who
soon	go
up	for

say	make
new	play
said	them
good	give

all	was
she	then
over	ate
her	could

away	when
must	some
by	no
there	he

little	do
just	down
have	went
help	only

look	one
out	every
very	ask
their	walk

our	saw
day	put
too	take
show	off